A Praise-Filled Life

33 daily devotional messages
to inspire the Christian believer
into a deeper faith

Dedication

This book is dedicated to my two precious daughters,

Sarah and Heather.

Your love will always be my very heartbeat. I love you
both so very much!

Also, I dedicate this book to my grandson,

Blain Aaron.

What a joy you are in my life! I will always pray for
God's blessings in your life.

And finally, I dedicate this book to my parents,

John and Dorlene

I love you, Mom and Dad!

Contents

Introduction

As in my other books, here you will find proclaimed the Supreme God and Ruler of all to be the great I AM as revealed in the Old Testament. His name in Hebrew is YHWH (we would pronounce it YAHWEH should we be bold enough to speak His name). In Greek, His name is pronounced Jehovah. In English, we simply call Him God or LORD and one day He became flesh and bone in the person of Jesus of Nazareth. He was crucified on a Roman cross to pay the death debt of sin in our stead. He was buried and then rose again to offer us a new life through our faith in Him. Thus, He proved himself to be our Savior.

It is my hope that you find this book to be another resource for your time of personal Bible study and devotion. I hope it is a place where you find words of peace and rest for your soul. It is a place where you will find words inspired by the Holy Scriptures of God—His one and only written Word—The Bible.

Furthermore, it is my hope that the words in this book challenge you into a quest for a deeper and richer faith. After all, that is what Jesus wants of us, to live in faith. Remember, Jesus asked the question whether or not He would find faith on earth when He returns. The implication of that question is that He obviously wants to. So it is up to each of us to walk in that faith, to grow in that faith, to put it into practice, and to encourage others to do the same.

A Praise-Filled Life

With that in mind, I offer these devotional messages in the hope that your faith might be strengthened and enriched, becoming a deep well of God's grace from which you receive daily blessings as you seek to honor Him. Search the Scriptures often then. Pray unceasingly. Meditate frequently. Seek His direction in your life, and allow the messages in this book to help inspire you to continue practicing these things faithfully.

May your heart be richly blessed by God's love and grace. And may the words within this book help you faithfully follow Christ as the first and foremost goal of your life.

Agape,
Ron Dougherty

A new song of the heart

Reference Scripture: Psalm 96

How long has it been since our hearts have been found singing impromptu songs of praise to our God? How long has it been since the splendor and majesty of the holy Lord of heaven and earth has moved us to natural, abundant, true gratitude and thankful praise? How long has it been since nothing but humble adoration flowed from our lips when we consider His great love for us?

Truly, I must confess that it seems too long for me. Even a moment spent otherwise is too long, but my lapse has been greater than just a moment. Oh, sure, I enjoy listening to other people sing praises, and I sing along. Sure, I am often moved by their deep sentiments reflected in their songs as I listen to them on my favorite radio station (that's KLOVE in case you were wondering) and my heart can do little else but be moved to join in the singing. Still, the last time my heart led the praise was more than mere moments ago. Far more... And the last time that I sung the improvised words of a great praise chorus that my own heart composed—well, that was a while back, too.

Why? Why is my heart not moved to praise our glorious God in heaven in a new way every moment of the day? Why would I not humbly bow in reverence and raise my heart and hands in genuine adoration to the Lord of Lords and the God of creation, my Creator and Sustainer, all the while pouring out my heart to him? No, the greater question is why He loves me so much even though I lack such rich and heart-felt devotion. Yet, the truth is that He really does. As distractible as I am and as uncreative as my heart can be, He loves me still. He loves us all still!

What a mighty God we serve, as the old hymn says. What new song does my heart sing today? What a mighty God I serve! He is wonderful and full of wonders beyond my greatest contemplations...My God, the healer of my soul, the source of my joy...My God, who holds the universe in His hands, my friend, my Savior...

What does your heart sing today?

Have a wonderful day in His grace!

A simple thank you?

Reference Scripture: 1 Timothy 1:12-17

Paul said that he thanked God that He considered him faithful and called him into His service, even though he was once a blasphemer and a violent man. In this letter to Timothy, he had just written about the difference between the Law and the Gospel of Christ. The law was made for law breakers. That's what Paul was. He was a blasphemer. He was a sinner. The law was made for lawbreakers...to punish them. But grace overcomes the law with forgiveness. "I thank God", he said, "that He considered me faithful. "If we think about it, it's a reminder that even while we were yet in the practice of sinning, Christ Jesus came into the world to save us (read this for yourself if you want a firm reminder...Romans 5:8).

We often are reminded that grace is not depended upon merit. We can't earn grace. We don't deserve it. It's not a result of our good behavior. Otherwise, it is not grace, but a reward. Paul realized this deeply. So he thanked God that God chose him...that God considered him. Do we? Do we thank God and humbly and sincerely thank Him that He chose us? Do we appreciate the fact that He considered us? Is it among our thoughts to honor Him? In His infinite goodness and greatness, He had the mercy to look upon us (even though we are flawed and sinful creatures) and had mercy on us! There was no reason for Him to do so. We didn't deserve it. We could do nothing to deserve it. Yet, He looked down upon man—at you and me—

and in essence said to Himself, "I love this person and I want this person to be with me. Therefore, I will do what it takes for this person to have a relationship with me."

Do we thank God for this? Does it mean anything really to us? If we fail to thank Him, then do we fully realize all that He has done for us! He did it ALL because we could do nothing. Is it important—urgently important—for us to consider that everything that was done to offer us salvation and a new life was done at His expense, not ours. It was God's will not ours. We deserved nothing but what the law would have brought us. Death. But instead, in His grace and mercy He offered us life. Yes, we ought to thank God! When we offer a gift to someone, and that person doesn't even say a simple thank you, are we not likely to feel as if we should not have even bothered? No one I know appreciates ingratitude. Even a simple acknowledgement goes a long way. Right? What about the gift of Life, then? What about the gift of God's love? What about the gift of an eternal reward in joy and presence of the Almighty? Are these not worth at least a simple thank you? Of course they are! They are worth so much more! They are worth a true, dedicated, heartfelt response of gratitude and devotion to the One who offered such great gifts!

Have a wonderful day in His grace!

An inspiring prayer

Reference Scripture: Psalm 17

This prayer of David is truly inspiring. From the heart of a man enwrapped in not only the awesomeness of God, but His tenderness and mercy, comes this breath of life.

He prayed for the resolve of Job, that though he would be tested, he would be found faithful, declaring that he had remained faithful and would continue to do so. He vowed to place each step of his daily walk carefully, so that he would walk in the path of God. But he called on God to be his refuge and strength, knowing that he could not accomplish it in his own strength (and indeed, as we know David's story, he fell flat on his face when he removed his eyes from the goal and relied on his own strength). So, relying on the *wonder* of God's great love, he placed his full trust and assurance into God's hand.

"Keep me," he prayed, like a small child clinging to his father, who stands so much taller than he, begging to feel that fatherly affection and assurance. "Hide me," he begged, like the child who fears the coming storm and begs for his parent's protection.

Is that our prayer this morning? Are all of our cares and worries abated by the simple prayers of "keep me" and "hide me"? Are our hearts at peace as we await the *wonder* of God's great love to unfold in tender compassion and provide our refuge? Will our pains and fears be eased knowing that the Almighty God hears our prayers and loves us enough to answer them?

If these questions are not all answered with positives, then our faith is in vain. Is it not? Oh, but they all **can** be answered positively. He is the Almighty! He does love us! He promises to be our Comforter! He invites us to bring our burdens to Him! And He promises to be our peace! Our faith can stand firm, for it is in Him that we live and move and have our being...

Have a wonderful day in His grace!

Are you blessed today?

Reference Scripture: Psalm 33:1-22

In this passage the Psalmist made a very pertinent and often quoted comment. He said, "Blessed is the nation whose God is the LORD." Seldom, however, do we really look into the matter. You see, only when a puzzle is finally put together can the 'big' picture be seen. The same happens when the whole of this psalm is read together.

The psalmist begins with acclamations about the LORD (YAHWEH to the psalmist, Jehovah to the Greek translators, and we call Him God). He is faithful, true, worthy of our cheering and praising Him like we were in a stadium full of fans cheering and praising our favorite football team. In fact, far much more worthy than that! His love is for righteousness, i.e. always doing what is truly 'right', and He fills the earth with His love. He is the creator of what we see, the heavens and the earth. He filled the oceans with water and could scoop them up again with His hands. He is so great and awesome in power that no man could overpower Him. Simply through His speaking of the word our world came to be! Then, even beyond that, He is greater than all of the nations, individually or combined. None of them can do anything without allowance from God, for at a whim He could blow them all away with His breath like you might blow the dust off of an old book.

It is with this in mind that the statement is made that the nation who invites Him to be their Sovereign King would be truly blessed. Why? It is because this God, whose virtues and power have been explained, looks down upon mankind and considers all we do. He watches over the ones who stand in awe of His glory and delivers them from their trials, provides for their needs and protects them through trial and encourages them when they are weary. He becomes their strength and their shield of protection. He becomes their reason for rejoicing. He promises to be their God and dwell among them. Who would not like to have Him as their next door neighbor?

Yes, truly blessed is the nation...the community...the church...the person...whose God is the LORD! There is no greater power than His. There is no stronger person or being. There is greater love than His. Yet, though we are merely imperfect earthly beings, He offers all of His tender care and compassion and all of His faithful devotion to us that we might be called His sons and daughters when we believe in His Son whom He sent to save us. And His children we are!

Do you consider yourself blessed today? Make Him the LORD of your life today and He promises blessings for you! Live for Him. Live through Him. Live to honor Him. You will receive His blessing. Guaranteed!

Have a wonderful day in Him!

Authority to heal and forgive

Reference Scripture: Matthew 9:1-8

Which is easier to say? You would think that saying the words, "your sins are forgiven" would be easier. But Jesus knew the real answer. Sin is not forgiven with simple words, but through the sacrifice of blood. Jesus knew full well that the blood that would be sacrificed would be His. Yet, the leaders and teachers of the time did not understand that.

For the Son of God, who is the Author and Perfecter of our faith and the Creator of all the universe, healing the human body would be the easier thing to say and do. The earlier chapters of the Gospel of Matthew are filled with healings that Jesus performed. Still, the onlookers didn't realize that there was more to Jesus than just flesh and blood. He was a man who could heal with only a word as He walked around those dusty roads teaching about the reign of heaven in the lives of His listeners. He taught and healed everywhere He went— asking for nothing in return. Surely He must have seemed to be different than the others around Him. Indeed He was! He healed flesh and bone! The sick were made well. The lame were made able to walk. The demon possessed were delivered to freedom. And who really knows all that He did while He walked the roads of the Judea. But something we do know is that He said, "So that you may know" He had the authority to forgive sins, he healed once again. And it filled the onlookers with awe!

A Praise-Filled Life

The good news for us is that you and I can take heart! We know that Christ is able to do the things that we consider to be the hardest. He can mend the human body. But, even better than that, He is able to do what God considers to be the hardest thing. He can mend the heart. He can mend it from not just earthly pain and grief, but also from the stain and oppression of sin with a compassion and forgiveness that is complete, restorative, and life-giving. So then, whatever our need we can take it to Him! If He can do these things—in addition to creating and sustaining the universe—what is there that He cannot do for you today?

Have a wonderful day in His grace!

Cherishing the Lord

Reference Scripture: Psalm 66:1-7, 16-20

Shout and sing and praise God. His deeds are awesome. They are things that we ponder in awe and wonder. You know, little things like creating the world, breathing life into dust and forming man and woman, guiding His people with a whirlwind by day and a pillar of fire by night, parting the sea and a river, and all those other Sunday school tales. Name another who has done these things. Go ahead. Name just one.

No one ever has and no one ever will do the things listed above. But, even beyond that, God didn't stop there. He kept on preserving and protecting His people. He sent Jesus into the world, turned water into fine wine, and fed 5000 men (and only He knows how many women and children as well) with just a few small fish and a few small loaves of bread. He raised the dead and healed the blind and lame. He foretold His death and resurrection. Then He accomplished them both.

Come and listen! God has done so much more than even just these things. These are things we should share with the world. These are things we should cherish and proclaim. If we will, we will see His wonders even still. But, if we fail to cherish Him and His works, we won't see them at all. So, watch and expect for Him to show His glory and then proclaim it when we experience it! It's a far better thing to cherish Him and feel His acceptance than to feel His rejection because we have ignored Him and cherished His adversary.

So sing praise to Him today. Come to Him and see His mighty works.

Have a wonderful day in His grace!

Continue to Rejoice

Reference Scripture: Philippians 1:19-26

As we look at the first chapter of Paul's letter to the Philippian church, we see his reason for rejoicing was multifold. First, he remembered his friends, who cared about him, stayed in touch with him, and prayed for him. Second, he seemed confident that he would be reunited with them and would be overjoyed in that. Third, he was performing what he felt to be an extremely honorable task. That is, he was counted worthy to be imprisoned for teaching about Jesus Christ.

But, believe it or not, some despair lingered in Paul's heart over his circumstances. He said so in his second letter to the Corinthian church. To that church he said, "We were under great pressure, far beyond our ability to endure, so that we despaired even of life" (2 Corinthians 1:8 NIV). Still, as told the Philippian church, he knew that these troublesome circumstances "happened that we might not rely on ourselves but on God, who raises the dead. He has delivered us from such a deadly peril, and he will deliver us. On him we have set our hope that he will continue to deliver us" (2 Corinthians 1:9-10 NIV).

So, we find that Paul, in tough and dreadful circumstances, looked back toward the encouragement of his friends, recognized the reasons and results for his circumstances, and put his very active faith into the hands of his God. He knew his God was alive and able to rescue, save, protect, and preserve. Then, even beyond that, Paul knew that if God would preserve his life, he would continue on the same path he was already on—a path of teaching about Christ and suffering for Him. That, he said, was his life! Even though his soul yearned to depart and be with His Lord, he would fulfill his earthly ministry with rejoicing until he could finally leave the earth to be with Jesus.

Today, let Paul's example lead you through your tough times. If you are in need of encouragement, seek out your true friends. Then, strive to understand what you need to learn about your circumstances and who needs to benefit through what you learned. And above all, trust in your Savior's Spirit to strengthen and preserve you. Remember, He sent His Spirit to be your Comforter and Guide so that you will never be alone but will always remain in the very presence of Almighty God!

Have a wonderful day in His grace!

Don't Settle For Less!

Reference Scripture: Psalm 33

Throughout the ages and even up to the present, kings and emperors have set themselves up as gods and demanded that their subjects worship them. But there is none worth worshipping, save one. That One is the LORD, God Almighty, Jehovah, Yahweh, the Great I AM. He is the Creator. He is the Sustainer. He is the Provider. He is the One called our Heavenly Father and He is the One who promises never to leave or forsake us. He came in the flesh to earth in the person of Jesus and opened the way for us to have a relationship with Him. So it is fitting that we sing joyfully to Him! It is right that we praise His name. It is good that we honor and fear Him, for His strength is greater than anything we might imagine. It is our calling as believers in Him to honor and respect Him in all ways so that others can see Him through us and turn to Him themselves to seek out this blessed relationship.

So then, I ask today, who is your God? Is He the One who made the starry heavens? Did He pour the waters of the seas out of the palms of His hands? Did He speak the command and all creation take place? Can He preserve and protect you by His great strength? Is He your help and shield, the One in whom you place your trust? If not, then you've settled for something less than that to which you were called! You were called by Jesus into perfect fellowship with the God of Heaven and earth, Almighty God! In reality, settling for a God who is anything less than Jehovah is settling for nothing at all!

In Him our hearts rejoice as we trust in His holy name. And through that Name, have a wonderful day in His grace!

Eternal treasures

Reference Scripture: Luke 12:22-34

Treasure in heaven or below? Jesus told us that we are to lay up our treasures in heaven where nothing can destroy them. There they are eternal and free from theft and destruction. His message was not just that good works create treasures for us in heaven. No, the message was that wherever it is that we place our heart's devotion will become the treasures of our lives. Are our heart's focus and our life's purpose to amass wealth and possessions? Then those are our treasures. Our world tries to tell us that, "He who dies with the most toys wins." But, in reality, he who dies with the most toys...still dies! My pastor says that never once, in all of the funerals he has seen or conducted, has he ever seen a U-Haul truck full of the deceased person's possessions waiting to go with him. No, there is only a casket...large enough for the body alone and nothing else.

Where the heart is there the treasure is. The heart concentrates on the things that it deems most important and most valuable. Is the treasure that we seek *on* this earth? Then it is temporary. Remember, Scripture tells us that the earth one day will be burned up with fire, melted with fervent heat. If this is the case, then our "treasure" is not eternal. In fact, it is not a treasure at all. It is simply a loan. It will certainly be taken away on the last day of our life...if not before. But if our heart is focused on the eternal—the Eternal God—and the riches that He has in store for those who love Him then we have a real treasure in heaven. If our hearts are focused on the Eternal, then He will be our treasure!

That's why Jesus told the rich young ruler to sell possessions and give them to the poor. We are not to fixate on possessions and worry over them. That's why Jesus said that God clothed the lilies of the field and fed the birds of the air. Our heavenly father knows we need food, shelter and clothing. Those are the temporary things of this life. They are simple sustenance and provision, not treasures to long for! And God has promised to provide them! We don't need to spend our days worrying about them. No, our treasure ought to be eternal in nature. It ought to be in the Eternal, Immortal, only wise God, Wonderful Counselor, Prince of Peace, Mighty God, and Everlasting Father. Why? He loves us and wants us to live with Him in His eternal joy! Now that is a treasure! And that ought to be what our hearts long to fully understand. That's what our hearts ought to be focused on grasping. In doing so, we will lay hold of a vast, incorruptible, corrosion free, inexhaustible treasure!

Let's not focus on the temporary things of this life! God has promised to provide those for us. Instead, let's focus on the eternal treasure found in our God. For where our heart is, there is our treasure also...

Have a wonderful day in His grace!

Expectation or apathy

Reference Scripture: Matthew 11:16-27

What would Jesus say if He walked into our world today? What would He say if He walked into our churches? What would He say if He walked into our homes? Would He compare us (in any or all of those locations) to children beckoning to their friends to sing and play and dance or to mourn and weep, only to find that the friends simply are not interested in doing either of the two? Would we be so disinterested in Christ's visit that we would show neither excitement, nor remorse, but only laziness and indifference? Surely, He would find us awaiting His return with expectation and anticipation, right? Surely, He would be greeted by our warm welcome and humble adoration! Surely...

But would He?

Friends, how could we ever remain indifferent to Him? Would it not be a much better thing to wait, in either sense of the word, on Him? We are told that those who do "shall renew their strength; they shall mount up with wings as eagles; they shall run, and not be weary; they shall walk, and not faint" (Isaiah 40:31 ASV). Christ's joy will be in our hearts! He will make our joy complete and overflowing and we will remain in His love if we will follow His commands (John 15:10, 11). There is no great feat of faith there. There is nothing of which to fear in following His commands. However, should we not commit ourselves to Him, and refuse to be changed by the love that He came to show us, He will tell us to depart from Him, because He never knew us (see Matthew 25:41). If we fail to be changed or to commit ourselves fully to Him, we will cause His stomach to wretch (Revelation 3:16). Then where will we be?

Jesus thanked the Father in heaven, Almighty God, that the secrets of the Kingdom of Heaven had been revealed to 'little children'. Like little children is how we are to accept Christ! A child is highly likely to believe something if it is told by a respected adult. That child will believe it and latch onto it as if it is absolute truth and will not be swayed otherwise. Children are so ready and willing to embrace things that come from the ones they respect, even when the idea is illogical and far-fetched. A perfect example of this is that many children are taught to believe that a jolly man with a beard can enter a house with a bag full of presents through the chimney of a fireplace! A receptive child is what we must become like if we are to be saved (Matthew 18:3). Yes, this was the Father's pleasure to work in this way, just as it was Jesus' pleasure to reveal the Almighty God to us!

He has done so much for us. Why would we ever remain cold to Him? May it never be! He came to bring us joy. So let's live in that joy. He came to bring us an abundant life. So let's live in His abundance. Choose to celebrate His love today, tomorrow, and every day!

Have a wonderful day in His grace!

Grace for the worst

Reference Scripture: 1 Timothy 1:1, 12-17

Have you ever wondered why God chose you? We have read that Jesus said, "No one can come to me unless the Father who sent me draws him" (John 6:44 NIV). And we have been taught that if Christ is 'lifted up' He will draw all men to Him (John 12:32). But, why did God choose us, individually, to be drawn to Him in the first place. The answer is in the very explanation of the question. God chose us so that we can be an agent to draw *others* to Him. God granted us His mercy, forgiving our sins, so that we might testify of His goodness and compassion to others. And as a result, others will come to Christ as well.

Paul echoed this thought in his first letter to the young minister, Timothy, who was like a son to him. He explained to Timothy his past persecutions and violence against the believers and how he was once full of wrath. Seemingly, Paul (or Saul back then) had no conscience. Then God took hold of his life! Everything changed in Paul's life and word spread that the man who once raised havoc in Jerusalem trying to arrest the believers (see Acts 9:20) was now fully committed to the teaching of Jesus as the Christ, the Son of God and risen Savior. In recounting this to Timothy, Paul said that it was because of these things in his past that he was called into Christ's service, that he might proclaim that the very same mercy and forgiveness shown to him was available to everyone else as well. He felt that he was the worst of all sinners and that if God's grace could save and restore him, it would certainly do the same for anyone else.

Friend, that same grace is available to us today! And that same grace needs to shine through us today as well.

So why would God choose us? He chose us so that He could show His glory to the world. No, we might not have been as mean and wrathful as Paul, but while we were sinners (i.e. were still practicing our sins as Romans 5:8 points out) God still chose to offer us His grace. God took hold of our lives and now we too can say that things from our old lives have changed. Others have noticed—and will notice—those changes. Now, because they can see the changes in us, they may be drawn to God as a result!

Let that be our prayer today and have a wonderful day in His grace!

He is greatly to be praised!

Reference Scripture: Psalm 29

Why did David write this psalm? Some commentators say that he may have written it after a great thunderstorm. Some have said that the drought-breaking rain noted in the 21st chapter of 2 Samuel might have been the reason. Some say it really doesn't matter when David wrote it, only *that* he wrote it.

Regardless of when or why, the point is clear. God is great and He is greatly to be praised! There is glory that He is due and He radiates that splendor on those who worship Him.

Yes, His voice is powerful enough to thunder and cause tumult over the seas! It was even powerful enough to calm them (Mark 4:39)! His voice is powerful enough to break great trees. Why not? That same voice created those trees! Why would it be difficult for Him to break them? His voice could shake the mountain range called Lebanon. Of course it could! At one point that voice separated all land from the sea and gathered it to where He wanted it! The voice of the Lord strikes with lightning! One translation says it can separate the flame tips from the fire. Sure! He once spoke separating darkness and light forever!

Yes, our Lord is a great God! We must never forget that and, in fact, must go even further than that. We must always *remember* that our Lord is a great God! That is an action verb! Daily that must be a part of the equation of our lives. He must be the focus of our heart's desire and the core of our very being. He sits enthroned over our lives, whether or not we recognize or acknowledge Him. He is there and His goal is the same now as it was in the beginning..."I will give them a heart to know me, that I am the LORD. They will be my people, and I will be their God, for they will return to me with all their heart (Jeremiah 24:7 NIV).

Are we fuzzy on who God is today? Are we unsure as to what He wants for our lives? Do we feel like we are alone in life? Do we wish we had peace in our hearts? Then we must ask ourselves who sits on the throne over our lives? Are we taking someone else's spot trying to govern ourselves, thinking we have all the answers for our own lives? It is quite obvious that no man or woman has all the answers to the questions of life. But the Creator of all life does. And He is the only One who does!

So I urge us all to ascribe glory to the LORD today! Lift up His name in the highest of reverence and honor Him above any and all else! He alone is worthy of our praise. He alone...

Have a wonderful day in His grace!

His Majestic Name

Reference Scripture: Psalm 8:1-9:1

What is man that the Creator takes notice of him? What is man that the Almighty God would look down from heaven after creating the universe, the mountains, the seas, and all of the creatures on and within them, and then think of him? Who are we, that the Almighty has any interest in us at all?

We are His people. That's who we are. We were created to be like Him in creativity, imagination, reason, intellect, and in many other ways. Originally. No, mankind is not godlike. Nor will we ever be. We cannot attain such lofty aspirations in our lowly, earthly, selfish, sin-stained flesh. But our God sees beyond that when we call upon His Son, Jesus to be our Savior. He sees us as members of His own family. He sees us as ones to be protected and sustained. He sees us as heirs of His righteousness and godliness, through the living out of our faith in Him. He looks beyond all those things that would separate us from Him, and instead, sees us as His dearly beloved children. That's who we are that God would be mindful of us.

Then, the question must be asked, who is God that we should be mindful of Him? He is GOD! Creator. Provider. Sustainer. Guide. Protector. How many more titles could be added here? I'm sure there are countless ways to describe Jehovah, God Almighty. Those are only a few statements of who He is! So it is right that we should be mindful, respectful, and full of awe that He notices us. Even better, He goes beyond just noticing us! He cares for and nurtures us daily, giving us our life's breath, daily provisions, and life to our souls. Our God is the King of Kings and Lord of Lords! We ought, therefore, to meditate upon this and joyfully respond to Him with an offering of our lives to Him and submitting our will to His.

May your heart overflow with His love today, that you might proclaim, "O LORD, our Lord, how majestic is your name in all the earth!"

Have a wonderful day in His grace!

His prayer and purpose

Reference Scripture: Matthew 3:13-17

Many men have played incredible roles in the formation of civilization. Many men developed philosophies and religions to assist others find their own way as they walk on earth. Many men have attempted to tame the human spirit seeking to attain a higher level of existence. But, how many of these figures in history were specifically endorsed by direct and public proclamations from heaven? Wait...how many did you say? ONE! Yes, only one. His name was Jesus of Nazareth. He was proclaimed the Son of God by the voice from heaven above. This was witnessed by those in the crowd around Him that day. It was also testified to in writing and has also been testified to by countless thousands of individuals who have been touched by His life of agape love on their behalf. He alone is the Way, the Truth, and the Life, and no one comes to the Father, except through Him (see John 14:6).

He was not just a man who stood out from the crowd because of this proclamation. He was God who came to earth in the form of a man. He came as our Savior. He came on a mission! He came with a purpose. In John 17 we can read His own stated prayer and purpose: "Holy Father, keep them in your name, which you have given me. Then they will be one, just as you and I are one...I do not ask you to take them out of the world. But I ask you to take care of them, so that the evil one of this world will not harm them. They do not belong to the world, even as I do not belong to the world. Make them clean by the true word and keep them for yourself. Your word is true."

He went on to say, "I have sent them into the world as you sent me into the world. I have made myself clean and kept myself for them, so that they may be clean and be kept for you also by the truth. I do not ask this for these people only; I ask it also for the people who will believe in me when they hear what these people say. I do this so that the people will all be one. That is the same way with us. You, my Father, belong to me and I belong to you. I ask that they also may be joined to us. Then the world will believe that you have sent me" (John 17:11, 15-21 World Wide English translation).

I will add no further commentary to those words of our Lord. I do hope, though, that your day may be filled with awe and wonder that the Son of God *planned* for you to be part of His life...forever!

Have a wonderful day in His grace!

I will sing praise

Reference Scripture: Psalm 104

Once again the psalmist calls out the glory of God. His understanding of the greatness of God was sure. His knowledge of the wonders of God was great. He would continually praise Jehovah for His majesty and awesome strength. From the depths of his soul, the psalmist rejoiced in the Lord and from the core of his being he praised the God of the Ages. Why not? Who could fail to do so also once he or she would fully understand that our God is the God of Creation, the One who set the sun, moon and stars in their places? Who could fail to honor and praise the King of Kings who offers His lowly subjects every breath of life they take? Who would ever fail to offer the due honor and glory to the King who offers grace and mercy to His people?

Oh, I have so much to learn! Too often I am that one! I fail to praise Him. I am negligent in honoring Him. My humanity gets in the way, and I forget that He alone is God. He alone is worthy of all praise. He alone is the Supreme Power in the universe. He is the Giver of my life. Still, though I am negligent due to my human nature of selfish sinfulness, God remains ever faithful in His holy and divine nature of righteousness. He still offers His grace and mercy and loves me anyway.

Yes, it is true. He is a mighty God that we serve. He is full of wonders and majesty! Let us offer Him our praise today. Let us offer Him our devotion as He already has offered His to us. May all in the world be filled with His glory today. And may that begin within us!

Have a wonderful day in His grace!

In all we do...

Reference Scripture: Ephesians 5:15-6:9

True enough, Christianity is not a religion of do's and don'ts. It is also not a methodical fulfillment of regulations. It is, instead, the response of the believer's heart to the love of God that prompts the genuine actions of Christ's unconditional love. We are to live as "children of light", open and transparent to those around us. That way everyone will see that the reason we exist is to bring honor to God through Christ.

Whether we are in conversation with others or business dealings with them...whether we are learning to live with our wives or husbands...whether we are children under the influence of our parents or parents raising our children...whether we are employees of others or the employers of others...we ought to live wisely and act appropriately for the sake of the name of Christ, who is our Lord. Everything we say and do enlightens the world to how we do—or do not—honor and reflect Christ to the world.

- If today is full of weakness, then ask Him for strength.
- If today is full of successes, then ask Him for humility.
- If today is filled with sorrow, then ask Him for comfort.
- If today is filled with joy, then respond to Him in praise.
- If breath in your lungs at all today, then thank Him.
- Let His love and life shine through to all you meet.
- In all you do, may Christ be honored.

A Praise-Filled Life

In all we do then, may we be careful to live wisely, make the most of every opportunity, understand what the Lord's will is for our lives, be filled with the Spirit, speak to everyone with gentleness and joyfulness, and always give thanks to God the Father for everything.

Have a wonderful day in His grace!

Jesus on the street

Reference Scripture: Mark 10:46-52

How would we respond if we were to meet Jesus on the street in our home town? Would we chuckle to our-selves and make comments about His hair not being as long we thought it might be? Would we be surprised at the size of His nose or the breadth of his shoulders? Would we make eye contact with Him or look away in uncertainty? Would we poke fun at Him by asking Him to walk across a puddle without getting His feet wet? Or would we respond in the opposite manner with respect and some humble greeting as if we had just met some great world leader? Would we laugh and jeer? Or would we simply beg His mercy for our souls?

Bartimaeus was an interesting man. He was blind from birth and therefore unemployed. He could only beg for his living. I picture him with a small cup in his hand pleading with those who came by to drop in just a few coins out of the several they probably had. He wasn't asking that anyone give him a wealth of money, only a handout...just a token. So, when Jesus was nearing he pleaded with a simple beggars call, "Have mercy on me!" Perhaps he simply believed that Jesus would just drop in some coins as well. Maybe, however, there was more to his begging. Maybe he just knew in his heart that, if he just asked, Jesus would turn and direct all of the Almighty's power to his own eyes and heal them. But, surely he thought that it would be too great a thing to ask of One so great! Surely, this great prophet and healer would never turn His attention to him. Still...

A Praise-Filled Life

"Jesus, Son of David," he shouted, "have mercy on me!"

Jesus turned to Bartimaeus and poured out that great and tender mercy on him. Bartimaeus received his sight and saw the awesomeness of the Almighty standing before him! What is more is that he responded by following Jesus in grateful response.

So how would we respond if we met Jesus? May it be that our first plea to our God would be that He might have mercy on us, to strengthen us and make our ailments and heartaches go away! May it be that we would recognize Him for who He is and that we are 'helpless and harassed' humans needing His great strength for our salvation!

True enough, we probably won't just *happen* to see Jesus walking down our city streets. But even so, we daily live in His presence. Yes, every day we walk alongside His Spirit in every place we go. He is out on the streets of our hometowns, in the hallways of our workplaces, in our own dining rooms where we ate our breakfasts this morning. Indeed, know this, everywhere we have been and everywhere we will go today, He has been there and will be right there with us. As a matter of fact, He is standing next to you and me right this very moment. So, then, just which response will we have, "Lord, have mercy on me" or some other greeting of a non-committing and casual nature? Will we say a simple, "Hi, how are you doing? Let's talk some other time?" Or will we earnestly plead, "Lord, have mercy on me..."

Have a wonderful day in His grace!

Learn to do right!

Reference Scripture: Isaiah 1:1-20

Hundreds of years before Jesus came to earth this charge was leveled at Israel, the people of God. The Israelites were required by the Law and tradition to offer sacrifices at specific times and seasons. These sacrifices and the ceremony behind them were supposed to remind them of their guilt and, in turn, justify (that means to make "right") the ones who brought them. However, it didn't work out that way. People would go through the motions only, without paying full regard to the purpose and meaning behind the requirements. Theirs were hollow actions without meaning or real value in them.

Sadly, two thousand years after Jesus came to earth this charge can still be leveled toward the people of God, the Christians. We seem to go through the motions of our Christianity, sacrificing a Sunday morning to a church service and maybe an evening here or there to other church work, a prayer here, a song there. Like the Israelites, the meaning and purpose behind our faith and the requirement to love our neighbors as Christ loved us seem to get lost in the selfish distractions and pragmatics of our daily lives.

It is still true today, just as in the Old Testament times, that it is the true and faithful ones who please God. We are told that "without faith it is impossible to please God, because anyone who comes to him must believe that he exists and that he rewards those who earnestly seek him" (Hebrews 11:6 NIV). Since the time of Cain and Abel, God has never, and never will, be interested in practiced and meaningless sacrifices. The motives behind them must be genuine, heartfelt, humble and complete.

So, let us learn to do right! Even more, let us practice it out of response to God's love, with a pure heart and clear conscience. In that way we will accomplish our purpose here on earth...to bring glory and honor to the name of Jesus, the Christ, and God Almighty, the Great I AM!

Have a wonderful day in His grace!

Never distracted...

Reference Scripture: Philippians 3:7-1

What passion Paul expressed in this passage from his letter to church of the Philippians! He had given up everything that he had worked for prior to his conversion to Christianity. Why? The surpassing greatness of just knowing Christ Jesus made the worth of everything else in his life fade away to the point of worthlessness. That's why!

You might say that he acted foolishly. Many have. Still, Paul loved his God so much that he wanted to truly know and understand the mind of the promised—and delivered—Messiah, Jesus. He no longer cared about the self-righteousness that he once sought to obtain as a member of the Pharisees, which was a strict religious sect of the Jewish nation. His heart-felt goal was to know the wealth of knowledge and the breadth of righteousness that comes only from God Himself. Nothing else mattered in his life but these things. In them he would *know* the power of Christ's resurrection. And in following Christ's example he too could experience the working of the Almighty's great power that brought Jesus out of the tomb.

So, what motivates us? Many of us have come to Christ out of a personal need. We were burdened and, in coming to Him, we found that He cares for us enough to remove our heart's burdens. So we turned our hearts over to Him. Others of us have turned to Him to escape the lake of fire awaiting us if we die without repenting of our sins beforehand. Others of us have grown up around the teachings of Jesus and have understood and accepted their truths our whole lives. All of these are good reasons to turn our hearts over to God. But, what is our current motivation to *continue* on? What causes us to believe *today* in the righteousness that comes through faith in Christ and in the power of His resurrection? If we have no ready answer, then our hearts may have become distracted. Peter wrote that we must in our hearts "set apart Christ as Lord...[and]...Always be prepared to give an answer to everyone who asks [us] to give the reason for the hope that [we] have. But do this with gentleness and respect, keeping a clear conscience" (1 Peter 3:15-16 NIV). We must then, see our faith with the focus and passion of Paul that he showed us in the reference passage above.

Let us never become distracted from the one thing in our lives that truly deserves the passion of our hearts. May the reasons for our belief in the Son of God, Jesus, the Christ—Almighty God in the flesh—be first and foremost on our minds, ready to be offered for the asking. And may those reasons prompt us to complete, faithful and diligent service to our God and King!

Have a wonderful day in His grace!

O LORD, my strength

Reference Scripture: Psalm 18

This psalm begins with this description, "Of David the servant of the LORD. He sang to the LORD the words of this song when the LORD delivered him from the hand of all his enemies and from the hand of Saul." King Saul was chasing him to have him executed, so David was on the run and hiding out in caves. He was like a hunted animal, hiding in fear for his life. What else could David do but pray and cry out to his God? The story though, grows brighter in the outcome. David was spared. Saul did not kill him. David felt the strength of YAHWEH, the LORD Almighty, when he survived the attacks of his enemies. So as a result, he penned the words of praise in this psalm.

Have you been armed with strength for today? Are your feet swift and steady as a deer's? Are you standing on top of the things that are trying to bring you down? If not, then let these words from David help you find the power that God offers to those who believe on Him! He found that God hears His people when they cry out to Him. He found that God helps those who cry out to Him, not those who help themselves. He found the living God Almighty is not only able to deliver and sustain, but also able to love and pour out compassion. You can know these things, too.

Maybe you know God's strength. Maybe you have felt it. Praise Him if that is so! You have seen miracles. You have been touched by the Almighty! And if this is so, maybe these words are for you to share with someone else that you know. Share your experiences with them, because they might be in a time of great need right now. If you help strengthen them in their time of need, you may have someone to help you through the same in the future.

Have a wonderful day in His grace and don't forget to share His great love with those around you!

Our testimony

Reference Scripture: John 9:1-7

Here was a man who was born blind. He could not work in society to earn an income. He had no disability insurance or other government assistance to provide for his family either. So, he had little option but to beg for handouts. He surely had little hope or grand dreams for his future. He sat alone begging for the slightest bit of compassion from the total strangers who would pass by.

One day, while he sat alone begging, a crowd of people came by with a commotion that was very noticeable. Some distance away they began talking about him. They could see him, but he didn't know who they were. Still, they were talking about him.

Was he apprehensive as to what they were going to do? Did he fear possible ridicule? Did he fear that he would be humiliated?

Then one man said something that he almost surely could not fully understand. "This happened so that the work of God might be displayed in his life."

What did the man mean?

The crowd stilled.

Why? Suddenly the unseen and unknown man was putting mud on the blind man's eyes...

A Praise-Filled Life

Did he struggle? Was the apprehension built to the point that he was truly uncomfortable or fearful? Was his heart pounding to understand what was happening? Or was there a calm peace that something wonderful might happen? Had the commotion caused a heightened sense of anticipation that the blind man realized he was in for something grand?

The stranger told him to wash off the mud. Of course, he would...Who would want mud all over their face, especially when it was made from saliva? When he washed, however, something miraculous happened. He began to see light. Then he began to see shapes.

What was happening?

He had never experienced these sensations before. For the first time in his adult life, he saw his own hands, still dripping with the water he just washed with. He saw the other people, who just moments before were only sounds. They now had shapes and visible substance. Their clothes were colorful. For the first time ever he saw what wind-blown hair looked like and the color of the dust on the ground.

Who was the stranger who brought the crowd and made the mud? Someone said His name was Jesus. Jesus... the name means "Jehovah saves".

Perhaps the man thought, "Is that because He just saved me from my blindness? Maybe He a prophet? Could He be Messiah? He can do things no other can, so

He must be something really special." Surely a flood of thoughts rushed through his mind!

If this were you, what would have been your response? How would you have acted? Would you have jumped for joy? Would you have wept in exaltation? Would you have been overwhelmed? Would you have thought, "Who did this?

Yet, this is no simple Bible school story. It is the story of the absolute, unconditional love of the Almighty God touching a person through Jesus, the Christ. It is the story of one man. But, it is also your story. And it is my story. We were all spiritually blind, without hope or direction, until we were touched by our Savior. Jesus healed this man so that the work of God might be displayed in the man's life. His testimony became this, "One thing I do know. I was blind but now I see" (John 9:25). So, I share this story to ask this question. Is this our testimony? He touched us so that the work of God might be displayed in our lives, too. When people ask who we are, our answer should simply be, "One thing I know, I was blind, but now I see. I was hopeless, but through Jesus I now am full of hope!"

Yes, my friends, I was spiritually blind once. But now I see! How about you?

Have a wonderful day in His grace!

Praise YAHWEH!

Reference Scripture: Psalm 150

"Praise the Lord" in Hebrew is "Hallelu Yah". It's a phrase that literally means *praise* (Hallelu) *YAHWEH* (Yah, is shortened from YAHWEH). The name of our God is YAHWEH in Hebrew. When Moses asked Him who He was, God said His name was YAHWEH, which when translated into English literally means 'I AM that I AM'. The Greek translation of YAHWEH is Jehovah, but in English, we just say LORD, or God.

Regardless of how we say it, each time we hear or speak the words "Hallelu Yah", we should recognize that we are saying or hearing words of praise to God, using His name. Any way it is spoken, His is a name not to be used in vain or in casual flippancy. If or when we speak it aloud we should understand that we reference the God of the universe, Creator and Sustainer of heaven and earth, who alone is to be praised.

Remember command number 5 of the 10 that He gave His people in Deuteronomy 5:11 was, "Thou shalt not take the name of Jehovah thy God in vain: for Jehovah will not hold him guiltless that taketh his name in vain." Sure, that's an Old Testament reference and we live in New Testament grace, but that does not mean it is now okay to no longer revere our God. Surely not! It is right and pleasing to Him for His people to honor and stand in awe of Him. It will never be right to berate, belittle, or dishonor Him by using His name in any other way than to bring Him honor and praise.

A Praise-Filled Life

As we read this psalm, or the many others like it, let us remember that they were written by a person whose heart longed for comfort and strength that could come from only YAHWEH, Jehovah, God. As we read these psalms may our hearts be filled with the understanding of the power and majesty of the One who bears the great name of God. May we praise Him for who He is, and may we do it with all of our hearts, minds, bodies and souls...and in spirit and truth!

Have a wonderful day in the grace of the LORD!

Praise the Lord!

Reference Scripture: Psalm 146 and Psalm 150

These two psalms are just wonderful to read for encouragement and strength!

Why? Probably because they just remind us that our LORD (YAHWEH in Hebrew...Jehovah in Greek...God in English) is on the throne over the universe and we don't have to try to be the one in control! We never could be and never will be in control. So instead of being downcast and depressed, laden with the burdens of life, we can praise the LORD for His care and concern on our behalf! We can praise Him that He is in control even when we do not understand how. We can praise Him that He loves us even when we are unlovable. We can praise Him through the storms and trials of life and we can praise Him when full of joy as well!

The next time you hear someone carelessly abusing God's name with a casual and flippant exclamation of "hallelujah" (as so many are accustomed to doing) tell them, "Thanks, I do praise Him! He is great and worthy to be praised! "

Hallelu Yah this morning! Hallelu Yah this afternoon! Hallelu Yah all day, every day! Praise Him! Let everything that has breath hallelu Yah!

Have a wonderful day in His grace!

Praise to the Lord

Reference Scripture: Psalm 148

Can there be any doubt as to what the psalmist is saying in this psalm? Surely not!

Praise the Lord! Hallelu Yah!

To praise the Lord is our duty and privilege as the people of God. We have, after all, been chosen by Him, offered grace by Him, redeemed by Him, and loved by Him! His creation exalts Him. His people should too. God is great and greatly to be praised by everyone who knows Him!

Do you see sunshine today? It radiates His light and love that protects and preserves our world. Do you see clouds of rain and storm? They represent the water that all life needs and some of the forces of God's might which are used for His own purposes. Do you see oceans and the creatures therein? Do you see mountains and hills accented with vegetation or frosted with spectacular snow caps? Do you see animals, birds, trees, or people? Do you see anything? They represent the creative genius and might of an awesome God who is full of infinite power and yet attentive to even the smallest of microscopic details. As Paul said, "...since the creation of the world God's invisible qualities-his eternal power and divine nature-have been clearly seen, being understood from what has been made" (Romans 1:20).

So, praise your God today! If there is anyone or anything that deserves your praise it is Him! Rain or shine...literal or figurative...praise your God!

Have a wonderful day in His grace!

Praising through it all

Reference Scripture: Psalm 34

Let the afflicted hear and rejoice that there is a place of salvation and comfort! There is a strong tower of refuge into which the oppressed can hide. There is an oasis in the desert that the weary traveler can find rest. There are arms outstretched that the burdened can find a comforting embrace. It is in the arms of Jehovah, the Lord God.

Take the example of David. Learn from what the man after God's own heart found. Through most of his hard times and trials of his faith he never wavered. He knew his redeemer was the Lord. He knew that salvation was in God alone. When troubles hit he turned to his Creator.

Think back, however, and remember that David didn't always have his heart set on the Almighty. No, when things were all rosy for him, being the king of Israel and honored and revered by all, he forgot his need to rely on God. In a moment of the selfishness of his sinful nature he committed a great sin. And afterward he committed other sins trying to cover up the first. No, there was nothing special about David. He was just a man. He was a human just like us. He wanted to please God, but at times he made some wrong choices and practiced sin. Still, he learned from his mistakes and did not repeat them. After repenting of his great sins and pleading with God to give him a clean heart and a right spirit before Him, David could later write the above passage.

God's grace and forgiveness will do that for us as well. It will renew us and make us right with Him. And when we are renewed and our relationship with God is in good standing, we too will find that we can extol the Lord at all times, in the good times and in the bad. We can and will boast in the Lord that He is great and has offered us His tender compassion. We can shout out our thankfulness so loudly that other afflicted ones might hear and be drawn to our Savior. We can take refuge in Him and be blessed by doing so, for we will lack nothing, have no fears and will live in a peace that will be able to transcend all understanding.

So, come and glorify the Lord with me! Let us exalt His name together! Let the others around us see us living out our thankfulness to God while we pray that they too will be delivered from their burdens by His tender mercies. And when they are delivered, let's all praise God together!

Have a wonderful day in His grace!

Reassurance and encouragement

Reference Scripture: 1 Timothy 1:12-17

So often we neglect the fact that Paul, once called Saul, was a Jewish Pharisee (a teacher of the Jewish religious law). He was not only highly educated in the principles of the law, but also highly zealous for the power to protect them. He was so zealous for power that he had risen a place of authority that allowed him to imprison and punish those who acted in opposition to the Jewish law. He could convict suspected heretics and sentence them as a judge would do in a courtroom. So zealous was he that he had that authority to protect the Law to the point of bloodshed. The first Christian martyr, Stephen, lost his life through a public stoning while Saul watched and offered his approval. Saul was known for his persecutions of the early Christians. But, then he met Christ. His heart and life were forever changed. He would spend the rest of his life on earth travelling throughout the Roman Empire teaching about Jesus. He gave the rest of his life to proclaiming the Gospel, or Good News, that God loved the world so much that He gave His only Son to be the Savior of the world.

But, have you ever wondered whether or not his conscience kept trying to remind him of his horrible past? Surely, he felt grief in his heart at times for his heinous actions against people whose only crimes were accepting and reflecting the love of the Creator God. He called himself 'the worst of sinners', so he must have felt that remorse at times.

Still, however, he knew that he had been forgiven of his past by the same Jesus he had earlier persecuted. Jesus had cleansed him of the filth of his past, and Saul, who took on the name Paul, understood it well enough that he did not let it hinder his actions for the good. Paul's only desire afterward was to preach and teach about Jesus. He would later say, "Woe to me if I do not preach the gospel" (1 Corinthians 9:16 NIV). He also stated that his only reward was to offer the Good News of Jesus *free of charge* to his hearers and he lived in such a way that after he had preached to others, he would never *be disqualified for the prize* (1 Corinthians 9:27 NIV).

Remember, our past is gone in God's eyes if we have handed it over to Christ through confession and repentance. When we offered it to him He took it. And even if our minds or our Adversary still remember and remind us of what we used to be, God looks only at the faith living in our hearts—the faith, a belief that proves itself in action—that Jesus paid the debt caused by our sinful actions. God knows our hearts and offers us His Spirit to be our counselor, reminding us of His love for us, guiding us as we continue to live, and correcting us when we fail to follow His guidance. As a result, we can feel the same reassurance that Paul felt and taught almost 2000 years ago.

So, today, as we ponder again the reasons and results of Christ's work on earth, let's offer unto the King eternal, immortal, invisible...the only God...honor and glory, for He has done a great thing in our hearts!

Have a wonderful day in His grace!

Reverence and Awe!

Reference Scripture: Hebrews 12:23-29

Perhaps this verse comes to mind because of the earth-quakes that I've either felt or heard about here in Oklahoma and elsewhere through the years. Or perhaps it comes about just thinking about the awesomeness of Jesus as Emmanuel—God with us. Either way, this passage is worth our consideration.

The prophet Isaiah said in the 53 chapter of his prophecy, "He had no beauty or majesty to attract us to him, nothing in his appearance that we should desire him...He was despised and rejected by men, a man of sorrows, and familiar with suffering. Like one from whom men hide their faces he was despised, and we esteemed him not." And even though all of these things came to pass, Jesus was—and He still is—the creator of all things in heaven and on earth (Colossians 1:16). He is God Almighty who came to earth as an unimportant, lowly, unattractive human!

What a great picture this presents of His awesomeness! The Creator lowered Himself to appear as one of His created beings! The Almighty humbled and emptied Himself of His God-ness and became a man. How awesome must He be to do this! After all, He planned it all before He created the heavens and the earth and did all of this willingly!

How odd it is, then, that only on one certain day of the year—a day that we call Christmas—we celebrate His birth on earth. Yet He has given us His Spirit to lead, guide and direct our hearts and He is still very much alive and on His throne in heaven. Why is it then that we do not continue the celebration of His birth each and every day that He gives us life? It is never too early or too late! Let's celebrate the fact that He lives with us! Let's celebrate the fact that we can live with Him! You and I are in the presence of the Great I AM because He wants us to be there!

So, as the writer of Hebrews told us, let us be thankful and worship our God acceptably with reverence and awe (Hebrews 12:28). It is the only way to come before Him! After all, if He can shake the earth He is someone to whom awe and reverence are truly due. This is especially true given the fact that He put that awesome power down for just a little while...long enough to say, "I love you."

Have a wonderful day in His grace!

Simple truths

Reference Scripture: Psalm 9

There is a simple spiritual truth in this passage that ought to be remembered. Honoring the Lord ought to be where we place our focus and attention, while trusting and praising Him ought to be the goal of our lives.

The center of focus of a Christian's life is never to be on himself. A believer in Christ—if he or she really believes—ought to be on responding to the Lord's salvation, grace and mercy with a deeply respectful, joyful and thankful heart. No believer who understands that it was Christ's death on a cross that paid the penalty for his sin will ever overlook the cost paid by our dear Savior. The believer who recognizes that Christ's burial in a tomb is the burial of the old sinful nature to which we were once bound will never allow himself to be bound to that nature further. The believer who remembers the new life that Christ's resurrection offers us will never use that life as a license to wallow in the same sinfulness that Christ died to conquer. The believer who responds in true faithful devotion and thankfulness to Christ will find that his focus of attention will be on bringing honor and praise to his Lord alone, not on what reward may be found for himself...either now or later.

The heart cleansed of sin will be a heart full of gratitude. The spirit renewed will be a fountain of praise. The life restored will be a spring flowing with thankfulness and joy. The believer who has met with the Lord, humbly bowing and repenting of his sin, should never fail to remember that he has been saved through grace; the marvelous, infinite, matchless grace of our loving Lord. It is that believer who will tell of the wonders of God, sing of His praise, and speak of His majesty. And he will do all of that while standing in awe that the Immortal, All-powerful God would share His eternal life of joy with him!

The message behind this simple truth is this: God is God. He is majestic and glorious on His own. Man is man. He is worth nothing within himself. Yet, to God, man was and is worth every great and glorious thing that He is.

The question for today, then, is why is it so hard for man to say that God is worth the little that he is?

Have a wonderful day in His grace!

Sing Praise to the Lord, the Most High God

Reference Scripture: Psalm 9:1-10

You know, the Almighty God is still on His throne, working miracles and wonders. Each time you see someone give his or her life to Christ, you can rest assured that a miracle has been received. When disaster strikes, there are always miracle stories of heavenly protection and guidance. Even beyond all that, just a moment ago you took a breath. That was a wonder! And you just took another one. You awoke this morning and the sun still lit your world, even if it did so above a cloud covered sky. His wonders abound...if we look to see them.

It stands to reason, if this be the case, that those who know of God's name will put the trust that secures their lives into His hands. He is YAHWEH, Jehovah, the Great I AM. He is the One who is, always has been, and always will be what He will be. He is awesome in might and supreme knowledge, yet is tender in compassion and mercy. He existed before man began to calculate time, will far exceed the days of man, and will exist beyond what we deem as eternity. He is the great King over all. He is above all! Yet His creation, which includes you and me, exists only through His powerful, yet delicate, sustaining grace. Yes, He sustains everything so that we might know we have not been— and never will be—forsaken!

If then, the rest of His creation speaks of His wonders, do we? Do we offer our praise to Him as our Creator, our Provider, our Sustainer, our Protector, our Guide, our Savior? Do others around us see Him when they see us? Not every one of us is a good public speaker. Not every one of us has a bubbly and out-going personality, full of charisma and charm, attracting others as we live out our faith. Still, each of us have a different role to play in the displaying of our faith to the world, and we all should be guided by one purpose. That purpose should be to live in such a way as to bring glory, honor, and praise to the name of Jesus Christ, before whom one day every knee will bow and every tongue will confess that He is Lord, to the glory of God the Father (Philippians 2:10,11).

Have a wonderful day in His grace!

Testing my faith

Reference Scripture: Psalm 47

Here some questions to ask ourselves:

- How often in "awesome wonder" do I consider all the works that God has made?
- Really, does my soul sing to my Savior, "How Great Thou Art"?
- How often do I stand in His presence amazed and crown Him with worship and praise?
- Do I really proclaim "Holy is He, holy is He?"
- How often do I "Crown Him with Many Crowns" the "Lamb upon the throne"?
- And when I do, does that heavenly anthem really drown out "all music but its own"?
- Will I truly proclaim the "Fairest Lord Jesus" as the "Ruler of all nature"?
- And if I do, will I then truly say "Thee will I cherish, Thee will I honor, Thou art my glory, joy, and crown"?
- Do I see God as an "Awesome God"?
- Do I really believe that "He reigns over heaven and earth"?
- Will I really proclaim "Great is Thy Faithfulness, O God my Father"?
- Will I then be bold enough to announce "All I have needed Thy hand hath provided, Great is Thy faithfulness! Lord unto me"?
- And do I dare to state "To God be the glory, great things He hath done"?

- Will I honestly "praise the Lord" and again "praise the Lord" and really "give Him the glory" for the "great things He hath done"?

Do you see my concern here? I sing these songs on Sunday morning and enjoy singing them. They really uplift me and relax my soul. And well they should! They are songs that proclaim the awesomeness and the wonder of God. But I wonder sometimes whether or not I ponder His awesomeness outside of the church walls.

If He is awesome, then He is awesome wherever I am! If He is the Almighty, then He is the Almighty when I am at work as well as when I am in church! If He rules my life on Sunday between 10am and 12pm, then He ought to rule over me every other moment of my life. Otherwise, I belie the song...or I belie my heart. And if I belie the song and my heart, then I have shown my faith to be false. I would fail in the test of faith. I'd receive an "F" as a grade.

But it doesn't have to be that way! I can take that "F" and do something with it! I can take that "F" and put it at the end of "belie" and instead of belying my faith I can have "belieF" in the One I sing about! I can have belieF that my God is awesome! I can have belieF that my God is able to save me from myself and from sin! I can know that He reigns from on high! And I can proclaim Him as my Lord and Savior every moment of every day of my life!

The best part about it is that if I can do it, so can you! Stand and sing today! Let God be God and see His awesome work around you!

Have a wonderful day in His grace!

The discipline of the Lord

Reference Scripture: Deuteronomy 8:2-5

After the Israelites were led through the desert by God for 40 years, Moses began to teach them of the importance of paying attention to God's presence in their lives. Thousands of years later, this message is still very meaningful to us. We must remember how He provided for us in days past so that we will trust Him in faith that He will continue to do so in the future!

There is another point this passage brings up. God tests our hearts. Why? It's easy to say that He does so because He loves us. And that is absolutely true. Then why did He cause the Israelites to wander for 40 years through the hot desert of the Arabian Peninsula? Discipline is the answer. The nation had failed to obey God when He told them what they must do to inhabit the beautiful land that He promised to give them. So He disciplined them. Never, though, did He leave them alone, because He loved them too much to do that! He protected them. He led them. He gave them water to drink. He gave them food to eat. He even preserved their clothing. (Could you imagine wearing the same clothes for 40 years?) Then, at the end of those 40 years, after the discipline was over, He reminded them of these things.

If God tested our hearts today, would He offer reward or discipline? The truth is that we are tested every day. We should never fear when the tests arise to challenge our faith! These come so that our faith, which is of greater value than any amount of money, can be refined and that we might be found with a pure heart following the example that God laid out for our lives. If our hearts are distracted and our faith is weak then we should accept God's discipline and learn from His counsel. Don't despair that God might withhold blessings due to our lack of faith. Just as children are disciplined by their parent for disobedience, so are we by our loving heavenly Father. Seek to honor God and His blessings are promised to follow as a reward. If, on the other hand, we are found with a clean heart and healthy faith, then praise the Lord that He has guided you well to your reward...only now turn around and pass the blessing on to those who follow behind you!

Whether we walk in trial or discipline or blessing today, may we walk in His ways to bring glory and honor to His Holy Name!

Have a wonderful day in His grace!

The imitation of God

Reference Scripture: Ephesians 4:22-5:2

Be imitators of God through living a life of love. Paul can be no clearer on this point, showing that Christ is our example of devotion to God. Paul's statement follows a listing of teachings on what to "put off" from our former ways of life. Those things are contrary to the practice of unconditional, agape (Godlike love) and therefore, ought never to be found in the believer's heart and life. Corrupt, deceitful desires cause one to practice falsehoods, angry outbursts, stealing, unwholesome talk and other things. These are wrong for a Christian to practice. Actions that grieve the Holy Spirit of God, like bitterness, rage, brawling, slander, and malice should also not be practiced in the believer's life. Instead, kindness, compassion, forgiveness and the practice of agape ought to be the actions prompted by the faith of the believer.

Why should we live this often-times difficult life of unconditional love? There are several reasons. First, we should love because Jesus of Nazareth loved us enough to die for us and if we call Him our Lord, we ought to follow His example in order to please Him. Second, we should love because, as the apostle John tells us, God is love and whoever does *not* love does not even *know* God. So, the practice of love is the indicating factor of who knows God and who does not. Thirdly, we are *commanded* by Jesus to love. John 15:12 records Jesus' words in this way, "My command is this: Love each other as I have loved you." No amount of explanation could make this point clearer. No interpretation or commentary needs to be added. It was a command by our Lord Himself. To remain in Jesus then, from His own words, requires that we must live lives of unconditional love, just as He did.

Still, there is one more point to make from the above passage. We are to imitate God as dearly loved children. We *are* dearly loved children! So, just as my daughters seek to imitate my ways because I am their example and guide, we should be looking to God through Christ to follow His example and guidance...as His dearly loved children. The Great I AM, the Creator of the universe, the Giver of life, the Father in heaven loves you and me as His dearly loved children. That is reason enough to respond by living a life filled with the practice His love.

Have a wonderful day in His grace!

Token acknowledgment or total surrender

Reference Scripture: Romans 1:18-25

It is quite obvious that Paul believed that God was undeniably present in both the creation and in the ongoing preservation of what was created. God was the Power that controlled the universe. No other power was His equal and no other presence but His deserved glory and worship. Furthermore, to Paul, man was a created being that was not worth worshipping. Everything else, including images and idols, was made by men who were themselves created beings so they were not worthy of honor or worship either. To Paul, only the One with 'eternal power and divine nature' was worthy of his devotion.

Should that not be the same with us today? What does this world attempt to offer us that has not been created by another created thing. What benefit beyond the grave will anything that has been created on this earth offer us? What exists on this earth that is not inferior to the Creator and Sustainer of our universe? Money? No, it's created in every country on the planet. Fame? No, it's created in the minds of lowly selfish created beings. Homes? Sporting stars or legends? Political figures? Business success? No. None of these things will last much more than a breath beyond our life's short duration. They are in all ways inferior to the everlasting Creator. So, why would anyone in their right mind worship and devote themselves to something which is virtually invisible in the scope of eternity?

What is the point of wrapping ourselves and our devotion around these things then? Since these things will pass away, what good will it do for us to devote our lives to achieving them? The answer is quite obvious. Nothing. Devotion to these things steals our affections from the only One who really deserves our devotion. We have been told that if we seek Him and His righteousness first in our lives that He will provide everything. Bear in mind that He also provides the righteousness that we seek, our fellowship with Him, and an eternity in His immeasurable joy as well. With these, we have the ingredients of absolute and true success. Stockpiles of money will not compare to those riches. Any number of homes or any amount of worldly fame pale in comparison to the joy of being welcomed into the home of God with the loving words, "Enter into my Joy," spoken from His own mouth as He ushers us in!

Why set our sights on anything less than all of this? Why sell ourselves short? The Author of the universe and the Father of our faith has invited us into His family just as we are. So why would we wish to drag along so much worldly baggage with us? None of it will enter into His joy with us. In fact, should we wish to drag it along, it may keep us from entering in if we cannot let go of it.

What is our excuse for not surrendering our whole selves to God? God has made Himself—His power, His love, His grace, and all that He is—plain to us and available to us. What more must He offer before we will offer Him something more than token acknowledgment?

Praise Him every day and have a wonderful day in His grace!

Don't forget to read these devotional
books by Ron Dougherty:

A Christ-Filled Life
A Passion-Filled Life
A Peace-Filled Life
A Power-Filled Life
A Prayer-Filled Life
A Spirit-Filled Life

Be encouraged and challenged

Made in the USA
Monee, IL
07 July 2026